Under the Same Sky

Under the Same Sky

poems

Carolyn Chilton Casas

2024

GOLDEN DRAGONFLY PRESS

AMHERST, MASSACHUSETTS

FIRST PRINT EDITION, August 2024
FIRST EBOOK EDITION, August 2024

ISBN: 979-8-9894116-3-4

Library of Congress Control Number: Requested

Printed on acid-free paper supplied by a Forest Stewardship Council-certified
provider. First published in the United States of America by Golden Dragonfly
Press, 2024.

www.goldendragonflypress.com

To my mother,
who pointed me to beauty in the world,
who reads more of what I write than anyone else,
and who pushed me to gather my poems into a book

CONTENTS

wherever we look, the chance for wonder

everyday holy

this shifting alchemy of existence

"Blessed be the longing that brought you here
And quickens your soul with wonder."

"For Longing," John O'Donohue

"To live in this world
you must be able
to do three things:
to love what is mortal;
to hold it
against your bones knowing
your own life depends on it;
and, when the time comes to let it go,
to let it go."

"In Blackwater Woods," Mary Oliver

Foreword

To Be in Love with the World

I read through *Under the Same Sky* during a rainy afternoon in Vermont, while wind tossed the maples and thunder rumbled in the distance. Yet, as Carolyn described the grounding force of the ocean and the swaying of palm trees, as her poems brought to life specific moments of everyday wonder, I was transported right there with her. It is hard to say what makes a poem, or a collection of poetry, succeed with its reader, but in the case of the book you now hold in your hands, I can say it simply: reverence for life. What Carolyn calls "a life-force so openhanded as heaven" animates every word on these pages. And while she does not ignore grief or difficulty, at every turn, she offers us a glimpse of daily gratefulness at work, what has carried her through the human journey so far.

As I read a poem like "Fortunate," for instance, about the unlikely miracle and risk of becoming a mother, I can't help but feel a certain stillness and attention gathered around her lines, as if they have always existed, and Carolyn has just coaxed them down out of the air we breathe. In the same poem, she writes of that young mother she once was: "Really, it's a leap in the dark / whether a single egg / of the four hundred or so / bestowed in her lifetime / will be in the right place / at the perfect time." I can't help but make the connection to writing a book and deciding to bring it out into the world, which is its own "leap in the dark" that carries with it a certain "euphoria" and "secret know-ing." The now living thing that you once nourished, one word and one breath at a time, is sent out to do its work, touching other lives, other hearts and minds.

Carolyn has also masterfully arranged these poems so that one leads seamlessly to the next, each one feeling gently inevitable, adding one more piece to the larger mosaic she assembles. For instance, the poem "After All," about preparing a meal in the kitchen with her aging mother leads to another poem about her mother, and another, and then "Our Daughter Asks," in which the poet's own daughter wonders about the secret of a long marriage. This happens repeatedly in the collection, and this deep attention to how the poems fit together to tell their story keeps the reader following the thread to the very end.

I also appreciated the way Carolyn has filled this book with actual, physical things drawn from everyday life to illustrate her message. In "Wise Words," for example, she meditates on her grandmother's losses and the lessons she imparted as a result. We then see the speaker of the poem unwrapping a pristine bar of soap she had been saving, and inhaling "the soothing / fragrances of peppermint and sage" as she decides to use and enjoy it. This seems one of the main intentions of these poems—to help us open our senses to the world just as it is right now. Don't wait, so many of these pieces say to us; revere the life that fills every plant, animal, stone, and human around you. *Under the Same Sky* shows us over and over how "to be in love with the world, / and when the time comes, release it."

James Crews
Author of *Unlocking the Heart:
Writing for Courage &
Self-Compassion*

Introduction

The Indigenous Chumash tribe of the California Coast—where Carolyn makes her home—holds dear an ancient cosmology that honors "sky people:" those who play an essential role in the healing of people, animals, the seas, the Earth. Occupying the "sky world," or *alapay*, are principal medicine-holders such as the Sun, the Moon, the Eagle, the Sky Coyote. Those who apprentice under such medicine-holders imbibe their healing qualities, their light. In this, her second poetry collection, Carolyn appears to have intuitively done just that: infused healing light into her poems, which, like prisms, extend beyond ecopoetics into the realm of the modern mystic, the lightworker, the spiritual healer.

The book's title *Under the Same Sky*, is borrowed from a grief poem in the second chapter addressing the ephemeral nature of everything under the sky, including our own existence. This death narrative stands in complementary contrast to the John O'Donohue epithet that opens the book: "Blessed be the longing that brought you here / And quickens your soul with wonder." For whether reflecting on losses or longings, exits or entrances, this poetry collection weaves a meaningful message throughout: that we are here to live in gratitude and wonderment, despite the inevitable brevity of all we hold so dear.

When first introduced to Carolyn's poetry, in the summer of 2020, I had just lost a dear friend as well as losing my beloved father. In my state of grief, these validating lines from one of Carolyn's poems comforted me: "You have borne the agony and the joy of impermanence. / Feel the coming and the going; / be exhilarated in the both." I knew that to feel exhilarated while grieving I needed to tap into the interconnectedness of all life, a theme in which Carolyn's poetry was well versed.

Like those who roamed the ancient California coast before her, Carolyn's poems reflect an intimate and very active connection with the Earth, the Sky, the Sea. Carolyn is practiced in living "deliriously in love with the world," even, and *especially*, during times of loss. For it is in letting go that one truly learns to connect with love's eternal nature. Beauty born of grief always leaves me in awe. How loss can produce something so healing is a marvel of nature in my eyes—perhaps even part of the "joy of impermanence" about which Carolyn writes. This light drew me in, and from it, a meaningful poetry exchange, Reiki apprenticeship, and special friendship emerged.

As a Reiki Master and teacher, Carolyn uses her hands as channels of healing energy. And like the five fingers on a hand, her book is divided into five chapters. The first chapter enthusiastically declares that we are all part of that healing energy; that we are made of light. Carolyn perceives this light everywhere and pours it into odes to the flora and fauna. When turning the pages of her collection, we gain a sense of the oaks, sycamores, eucalyptus, mulberry bushes, plumerias, and junipers that surround her—sacred in their own right. We are with her when she glimpses deer outside her window through bougainvillea vines, and for the rising and setting of full moons, Jupiter and Venus.

Like other healers around the world and across time, Carolyn participates in an ongoing dialogue with the life surrounding her: gophers, hawks, bees, hummingbirds, jackrabbits, and blackbirds. She writes about how we belong to the same tribe as "All of God's wonderfully wild creatures." This first chapter is full of wonder, miracles, grace. In it, Carolyn enthusiastically invites us to heal and become healers ourselves, declaring: "There are many ways to heal / one waiting just around the corner," and dedicates her work to "lightworkers the world over."

The second chapter plays with concepts of time, of past and present, eternity in the now. With flashes of life experiences, Carolyn takes us on a retrospective journey of her familial origins in Minnesota, where she planted a grove of pine saplings with her father at eight. And into the summer of '72 when Carolyn and her cousin were given tickets that, like magic, allowed admittance onto any ride in the park. Poems like "Autonomy" reminisce on growing up, picking out fashions with her mother, passing down her father's playing cards to her own children.

In poems dedicated to her children, Carolyn writes about the "euphoria" of motherhood after recalling the premature birth of her first infant. The last poems in chapter two follow a trial of loss and letting go. Thoughtful reflections on mortality at a reverend's vigil lead to acceptance. In "To Leave This Plane Gently," Carolyn writes

...there's no need to find a solution
to what isn't meant to be solved.
How useless it is, attempting
to thwart an innate process
wise beyond my understanding...

Tsunamis of unknowing,
portals to possibilities,
and the heavens quivering light.

The virtue of relaxing into a state of unknowing, while honoring the sacredness of things, illuminates the rest of the collection.

In chapter three, Carolyn gives us generous vistas of what stirs her soul: "fawns frolicking under the mulberries," spring "galloping" over velvet hills, Calla lilies and sheep calling out to her from across the fields. We hear about how light "filigrees the edges of leaves like halos." This verse, to me, reads like a cross between hymns, lullabies, and ancestral wisdom trickling through the author's close kinship with the Earth. Carolyn's practice as a Lightworker—her "way to love the world"—unmistakably palpable.

Whether loving the world through her hands as a Reiki Master, or through her verse as a poet, in each instance Carolyn describes herself, her heart, as a receptacle through which "creation's life-force" flows. Having entered her life simultaneously, Carolyn's relationships with Reiki and poetry are powerfully entwined. The two practices share similar characteristics. Describing her own creative process of writing, Carolyn wonders in awe at the mystery of the muse: how poems arrive, how they are captured, how they draw from her long bilingual relationship with words and language. Then, toward the end of the book, we almost predictably hear the author lose control of her poetry practice. Despite efforts to contain her experience, Carolyn surrenders to the unbridled playfulness of poetry, the surprise visitations, even the occasional teases that occur in dreams: "Try as I might to hold on, / words written in ephemeral ink / evaporate upon waking." Indeed, how does one hold onto light? And yet, her poetry does.

Carolyn's poetry is openhearted poetry. It gives in abundance because of its own receptive nature and ability to find fullness everywhere through a "luminous stitching / that binds together / calamity and good fortune," certainty and uncertainty:

There are so many things
I am unsure about,
but what seems totally clear—
I am not done opening
my heart to flower…

The paradox of fullness and emptiness existing simultaneously extends to the author's own existence, and how identity contains multitudes: aging alongside youthfulness, her ultra-achieving drive coupled with leisurely languishing in her garden, laughter contained in silence.

In "The Real Me" Carolyn takes an existential stroll through definitions of self, impermanence, negotiating linear time, breaking out of routines and habits—her life a snake that refuses to fall under her spell. The poems that follow move into philosophical questioning: What is essential? What is progress? What is clarity? Poignantly, the collection ends with a declaration of brokenness in "The True You." What do we do with all our broken pieces? And if we are, in fact, made of light, don't fractures just create rainbows?

Carolyn finds her rainbows in the "everyday holy," praising long summer days, the "temple of soft breathing," the "altar of oneness." With nature as her cathedral, she takes worship cues from the birds who even in a "questioning sky" sing openheartedly. As if returning from a long pilgrimage, with a heart full of revelations, the author's "pilgrim self" shares her own song "to meet each situation with kindness, show the world how we care, keep our hearts open reservoirs of love," extending gentle invitations to accept life "as it is."

Such poetry invites us to have conversations about faith, and what it means to practice acceptance. This theme rings through the collection as an intention that connects us to the otherworldly through our relationships to everything in this world. In Carolyn's experience of her own work, she writes "To my ear, every single poem / I write ends up / sounding like a prayer."

Reading through the poems in *Under the Same Sky*, I can't help but feel as if I am participating in a collective prayer, of sorts, led by an experienced healer—one of the "Sky people"—as it were, nourishing our individual sensitivity to the sacred found in every moment, to the divine light, to the everyday miracles appearing and disappearing under the same sky.

Catherine L. Schweig
Founder of Journey of the Heart:
Women's Spiritual Poetry Project

"You were born of a generation
that promised to help remember."

Joy Harjo, *Poet Warrior*

"Make visible what, without you,
might perhaps never have been seen."

Robert Bresson

source of light that you are

Ordinary Wonders

Waking is a miracle,
how the daylight
that greets us takes only
eight minutes, nineteen seconds
to get here from our sun,
zipping toward Earth
at a speed of 186,000 miles
per second.
And our bodies—
the mysteries we carry unaware.
They say we breathe
more than 20,000 times
in a day, and our hearts beat
ten times as often.
Think about how our legs
move us steadily
toward our desires,
the wonder of an open wound
closing itself while we sleep,
how our eyes can recognize
the light in the eyes
of another—
hold it an entire lifetime.

Becoming

Source of light that we are,
learning to appreciate
the magnificence of existence,

it isn't nothing,
the beings
we are becoming—

portals of possibility,
alive with such
innocent evolving,

grace in action
while life rattles away
under our feet,

spirits loosened,
growing
into our deepest desires,

gutsy enough to hold
our fingers to the gentle
pulse of the world.

Together in the Evening Light

In the soft light
of longer evening hours,
we sit down
at our rough pine table
with warm plates
of grilled fish
and steamed vegetables.
I glance past my husband
and see two deer
lying on the grass—
a doe, her eyes locked
with mine, and her fawn,
head twisted back resting
on his shoulder as he sleeps.
She does not startle
when I stand to bring
the butter, pour the wine;
they are frequent guests.
In a bougainvillea next
to the window, a blue jay
darts in and out,
carrying twigs to knit
her nest. Now she hops
in bushes near the deer,
then flutters to a stop
on top of the fawn.
When there is no complaint,
she begins to pick at his
molting hair,
his humble offering
to the blue babies
about to come.

What Opens My Heart

The play of light at any time of day.
The moon's cratered brightness

as it rises high above the eastern hill
behind our sleeping house.

All of God's wonderfully wild creatures,
especially those who share this land—

how the deer and lone jackrabbit
stop to look at me, as if wondering

if we belong to the same tribe.
The trees—the way steadfast roots

hold their bodies upright
in battering winds, how they offer

sheltering branches for birds' nests,
then watch over new hatchlings.

The ocean—the way it sends endless
waves as a message to not lose hope.

Best of all, witnessing unexpected bursts
of kindness makes my heart swell

to twice its size. Oh, what space is born
from the crazy grace of love!

What We Want

We want to be seen,
to be known,
to be valued,
to be loved—
for our visible splendor,
even more for our inner selves
and what some may call flaws.
We want to be accepted,
to be cherished.
We want connection
with each other,
with Mother Earth,
with whomever or whatever
we consider our Source.
We want to live in peace,
in radiant health,
the sun's warming rays wrapped
around us like a soft, thick shawl
against the unchangeable.
We want to create
something of meaning
from the depths of our souls.
We want to be valued,
to be loved,
to be seen,
to be known.

Knowing What We Know

What courage we must find
each morning
to open up to the world,
like a flower
exposing itself innocently
to hummingbirds and bees,

knowing what we know,
having seen
what we've seen,
the elements
that could cripple us—

blazing sun, stomping rain,
how in the chomp
of one hungry doe
the bud is gone.

But oh, how magnificent the bloom.

My Resolution

If the earth becomes a place
where we are not all
   wanted,
      taken care of,
         needed, and
            accepted,
I will change myself to light.

Light that colors your face
a rosy hue,
heals the wound,
helps plants grow,
allows all to perceive
the beauty of our world.

Light that shows the way,
dries up floods,
illuminates the golden specks
in your eyes.

I will make my way
into every darkened space,
even the tiniest of seeds,
filter myself through leaves,
create rainbows,
be your greatest friend.

How to Be in Love with the World

"Breathe in, knowing we are made of all this..."
"Eagle Poem," Joy Harjo

It helps to start with a curious mind.
Then, lace up your hiking shoes
and take to the temple of the hills.
Gaze anew at the landscape
as if you had just flown in from Uzbekistan.
You know, the way new arrivals
see everything beautiful
the first time.

Breathe in the untamed innocence of sage.
Pause to bow down
to tiny yellow flowers at your feet.
Tilt your head back to scan
for hawks' nests in the open hands
of lofty eucalyptus branches.
Soften your ears to a songbird
answering his love's call
from the opposite ridge.

See how you are a perfect piece of it all.
See how you can say yes to being the lens
through which a field of grace passes.

Then, oh then, you will feel what it is like
to be deliriously in love with the world.

My Intention

May the poems be like wind
in the tops of eucalyptus,
remembered long after,
even in the calm swells
of a still night.

May the poems be vibrant, like
the ring-necked snake last spring,
curling up the underside
of his bright red tail
so we'd take notice.

Especially, may the poems be
a dinner bell
to a table set for all
who care to come—
with dishes devotedly prepared
and bottles of red, red wine,
illuminated by the golden light
of many melting candles
and soft whispers
of close confidences shared.

Born Anew

I shall not lament
the splintered state
of the world,
not yet,
nor will I ever give in.
Where there is happiness
and love, forever
there will be hope
and light,
hidden, though it be
at times,
under a sacrifice
of adaptation.

If we are fissured by life,
we are fractured
like giant trees
scorched by lightning,
born into a new way
of being,
to an altered purpose—
a trunk hollowed out
to make a fox's den,
or mulch created
for the next
new seedling to take root
in the forest.

This Year More Than Any Other

Lately, in the mirror and close-up selfies,
I am startled to encounter
an older version of myself.
In my head, I am half that age.
Oh, to go back in time
to the smooth casing of youth.

This year, more than any other,
I feel the heft of gravity.

But then I reconsider, decide to
flip a switch and truly appreciate
my dear hands,
their healing power of touch
and how they write the words
that overflow from within.
Wide-open eyes,
that allow me to perceive
our world with never-ending awe.
Sweet knees,
for the strength to twist
and turn playing games.
A true voice,
carrying forth the beliefs I value most.
Faithful feet,
for taking me down
the planet's boundless paths.
And most especially, this perpetual heart,
with its guiding principle of love.

This year, more than any other,
I feel the blessing of being alive.

Beacon of Peace, Bearer of Light

for Tyann and lightworkers the world over

Thank you for being
the keeper of decency
and a way pointer for us all.

I bow to the everyday kindness
you humbly extend
to your fellow kind.

I feel your prayers
for a bewildered world
zipping through the air
from all ends of the earth.

I honor the unseen work
you do for humanity
behind closed doors, bringing
wisdom to soothe confusion.

Together we unite to serve one another
and in our purpose to create
a more loving place for our children
and for those yet to come.

With clasped hands we circle
land masses and oceans,
lighted candles of connection
emanating from our hearts.

The good we generate
illuminates, it beckons,
it makes all the difference.

My Creed So Far

Life is never-ending, death but a portal
to a new beginning.
Everyone and everything is connected
on an elemental level,
and it is possible to soften
into the potential of that unity.
There are many ways to heal,
one waiting just around the corner
for our awareness.
Responding with kindness
is the vital key to every difficulty.
Nothing, truly nothing, is more essential
than free-flowing love that is shared.

The Owls' Teachings

From beyond the darkened orchard,
I hear the blossoming calls
of a great horned owl
and his companion's reply.
From oak to pine, they converse
in a secret language
while I sit in between, guessing
at the meaning.

It's a blessing to feel their presence
though they can't be seen, and yet
with my closed eyes, I picture
their soft, feathered bodies,
heads swiveling side to side.

Could there be a teaching in this—
to open a space in my heart,
to consider them friends
for whatever time they are near,
until they take wing?

Oh, the jubilance among wild things!

An indigenous man in Guatemala
told me my spirit animal is the owl.
For a time after the death
of a loved one,
a barn owl visited at dusk,
bringing much needed solace
from another dimension.

And the clear message—
a cherished love between two beings
can never die.

Enveloped by the Tides

Everything shifts with the push
and pull of tides.
Wood, stones, glass get sucked
out, and the waves give back sticks
of smooth-edged driftwood,
pebbles to hold in our hands,
rounded pieces of colored glass.
Like the sea, I want to be open
for the world to pull me in.
What can be made softer
will be revealed
with love and attention.
What cannot be changed,
I will learn to release,
let it sink steadily
to my ocean's deepest ridges,
where the resilient things live.

Love Is an Imperfect Science

There is no perfect formula
that accounts for love.
No mathematics or proofs apply.

Take the exponential devotion of a parent
for their child—its geometry so compelling
we angle toward our offspring in wonder,

or the theorem of how we connect
easily with some strangers, not a simple
equation that adds up rationally.

Multiplication and addition
cannot sufficiently explain love.
Thinking about love as the principal factor

in forgiveness, can we count on
the probability of this logic
to calculate a much-desired release?

Love is a variable, the algorithm
unknown, an abstract
that calibrates in a nanosecond—

a shaft of heavenly light through trees,
the piercing eyes of an osprey
peering straight into my heart.

Life is not

to be taken lightly,
the sweetness of
its blessed wine
guzzled in a hurry,
but rather, it should
be cherished
with deep inhalations
of amazement
for its luscious aroma
and how lovingly
it caresses your tongue—
knowing at night's end
life's guiding lantern
will lead you home.

time's precious edge

Sometimes

Life gives you a morning
seated cross-legged, lotus pose
on the bedroom floor,
with a hot cup of coffee,
whipped cashew milk
and cinnamon stirred in,

looking out the open door
to wide-spread hawks' wings
circling the heavens,
riding their enraptured
roller coaster in the sky.

You spot a glittering
snail track, dotted like
the path on a treasure map,
woven between
fallen leaves on the patio.

And you feel happy
for the coming day, having
slumbered like an angel
in a cocoon of flannel sheets
and cotton blankets.

Life is like that. Sometimes
it gives you exactly
what you want and need.

My Place of Dreams

When I say *thank you*, I see myself
stepping out onto warm sand,
facing waves that greet me,
my legs and feet grounding
with our planet.
A soft breeze sways
through the tops of palm trees.
I soak in the smell of summer
and seaweed,
long days of light
with nothing needed of me
and nowhere else I would rather be.

The sea is my soul place,
a stage where I swim alone in dreams,
my skin breathing
in the sustenance of salt-laced water.
The ocean knows me
as one of her own,
a sea-child, a dolphin,
a pelican confident to dive
into unsounded depths.

Christened by cleansing breakers,
the beach receives me
to rest on its golden pew.
I sit embraced by the sun,
fingers shifting through mounds
of grains, the tiniest of shells
ascending to the surface,
gifts from Source
solely visible to the grateful eye.

I need to live near the ocean

after "I Need to Live Near a Creek," Hayden Saunier

because
the salty

smell
of seaweed

breathes
me whole.

Green Flash

The legendary green flash is real.
After more than fifty years
living on our coast
and countless sunset viewings,
I finally saw it,
as the last slice of ripe tangerine
slipped into
the horizon's expectant mouth.

I had thought it a tall tale,
much like merpeople
or mythical giant squid
sworn to drag down ships of old.

My friends also saw it.
Leaving the sand
where we'd played our games,
we stopped to watch
the barest visible edge
of sun being swallowed.
High-fiving, we shouted in unison,
It's real! I saw green, too!

Humble Praise

Thankfulness is a smooth,
  round beach stone
I carry in my pocket
and rub as a reminder
of all there is to be grateful for.
Today it's the one lone bird
who arrives outside my window,
    giving his all
  to usher in the dawn,
and my waking up eager
like a child for what
this impossible day might bring.

For the seven wild turkeys
  who show up
with their noisy gobbling,
their sounds sometimes heard
in the distant hills,
but never before on this land
    where we have lived
for nearly thirty years.

For the cactus that blooms
  giant ruby blossoms
only this month each year.
Sunlight soaks the petals through,
radiating prismatic hues
    of blues and purples.

And for the special grace
        of words coming
quiet as a whisper
in the middle of the night
            when I feel
I might never write again.

Half asleep, a thread to pluck
        and gently pull,
the lines unraveling one-by-one
into the open palm of my mind.

High in the Andes

In the main plaza of Cusco,
in front of the Catedral de la Virgen,
a celebration—Andean flute music,
Quechuan dancers in red and black skirts,

woven shawls, and bowl-shaped hats.
Women lead alpacas on leashes
down narrow cobblestone streets.
Under the shadow of a condor,

we are lifted centuries into the past
to ancient peaks and the Sacred Valley.
In an age-old hotel, they serve us
mate de coca for the altitude,

a tea for the vengeful *soroche*.
Nonetheless, like dominoes,
we succumb—one feels nauseous,
another lightheaded and short of breath.

Soon, the last friend, pale as limestone,
lays her head down on the dinner table.
In my single room, I am the final warrior
standing, but wake in the night

ears throbbing, head splitting,
heart beating out of my chest.
The next day, a much younger woman
is carried out of Machu Picchu on a stretcher,

and a young man falls face down
on the stones of Ollantaytambo.
Thus, the Incan gods of the Andes
continue to exact their revenge.

Soñé, Sueño, Soñaré

If I could go back in time
to have a heart-to-heart
with that skinny nine-year-old girl
wanting so badly to learn how to swim,
I'd say, *keep pestering your parents*
to let you take lessons.

One day, you will rescue a small boy
and a Catholic priest from the water,
then on a beach in Cabo, a woman
pulled out on a raging rogue wave.

Or the fourteen-year-old sitting
in her first Spanish class, conjugating
soñé, sueño, soñaré,
whisper in her ear—*You will be happy*
to have stuck with your studies.
Your destiny is to marry a man
who speaks Spanish, not English.

And then, the teenager with wanderlust
who hadn't yet traveled anywhere,
never on an airplane, or even a train,
keep dreaming, I could encourage—

You will fly in four-seater planes
across the border to help those
with no access to medical care,

free dive in the Aegean Sea,
canoe on a branch of the Amazon River,

31

watch the sun rise over the Himalayas,
swim from a boat off the coast of Brazil.

Indeed, it would be fun to go back
and tell her what lies ahead, but a shame
to deny those surprises on the horizon
beyond her imagination.

She dreamed, she dreams, she will dream.

Autonomy

My mother lost control of me at thirteen.
Long gone those short, pixie haircuts;
gingham and lace blouses
acquired from an aunt
who worked in a children's store;
and highwater pants
that marked me as an outsider,
my having immigrated
to California from Minnesota.

As I morphed into a teenager of my time,
I traded in my old look
for long, straight, loose hair;
fitted crop tops baring arms and shoulders;
bell-bottomed Levi's dragging
raggedly on the ground.

Babysitting allowed me to exert
my newly claimed autonomy,
provided money to buy a bikini
and purchase fabric
to fashion my own style of clothing.

We feel the need to create ourselves
in the image we see ourselves becoming.
That first beating of wings
against the cocoon that confines
strengthens us to fly.

Solitaire

for my father

The cards are worn, white edges
darkened by hands that often held them,
the numbers and letters
jumbo size for older eyes.
They no longer slide easily
like a new deck,
the bicycle-riding cupid
and his reflection faded.

On a visit home, my daughter asks
me to teach her Rummy.
Her boyfriend's family plays,
and she wants to take part.
I point her to the bottom cupboard
where board games
she and her brother played as children
occupy a neglected space.

These were Grampa's, weren't they?
She must remember
the many cribbage games
at the dining room table
after dishes were washed
or watching him play solitaire
nonstop in his small home on the hill.

When she leaves, I take the deck
tenderly into my hands,
shuffle the cards the way
he taught me, deal out
a solo game and begin to play.

Firsts

for my brother, Jim

There is a photo of us—he is twelve;
I am days old. He holds me
proudly, determined to be gentle
with the squirming infant in his arms,
his first sibling.

Years later, he came home
during a deep Minnesota winter
before shipping out to Vietnam.
There is a photo of him in uniform
next to a car covered in snow.
That visit, he took me on my first date,
my first movie in a theater—
The Sound of Music.
Afterward, we went to the only restaurant
in that small town, a truck stop,
also a first for me.
He wanted me to pick dessert,
so I timidly told the waitress
candy corn, a treat
I'd only dreamed about.

But now this—
the first time in my life
I cannot pick up the phone
and hear my brother's voice.

Wise Words

Looking for a hand soap,
I go to the cabinet, find
a special one I've stashed,
wrapped in green and white paper,
recalling it was more costly
than what I usually bought.

My grandmother's words
from forty years ago
suddenly come to mind,
telling me not to squirrel away
new things for special occasions,
but to use and enjoy them instead.
At a young age, she lost
a cherished older brother.
Walking on a city sidewalk,
he was struck down,
his head hit a brick, and he died.
Gone in an instant.
Her mother was never the same,
and my grandmother saw then
that items saved for a filigreed future day
are often set aside in vain
for a time that never comes.

Standing in the bathroom,
I hear her wise words
loud and clear,
remove the soap's pristine wrapper,
gratefully inhale the soothing
fragrances of peppermint and sage.

My E-Ticket Life

My cousin and I let loose
by our grandmother
for an entire summer day in '72.
How we coveted and cared for
those magic tickets, the green ones
in the front of the book
that allowed admittance
onto any ride in the park.

I've tried to live my life
like Mr. Toad's Wild Ride—
delight in surprises jumping out
around every corner,
daring, new detours waiting to
be taken, Fantasyland,
Adventureland, forays
into Tomorrowland's future.
Even the scary rides, like
the Haunted Mansion, endured
in the name of experience.

The only thing needed—
to remember I hold that E-ticket,
granting me first-class entrance
to whatever my imagination
believes is possible.

Bottom of the Box

So far, I've been lucky to live
a life I would perish for,

my everyday pockets full
of Cracker Jack surprises found

at the bottom of the box.
Having chosen to do what I most love

is one more reason to maneuver
through my days with awareness,

instead of checking off a list
that won't be long remembered.

I need a poem that gives permission
to disregard daily impositions,

tells me it's wiser to commune
with the sunshine, then with the moonlight,

a poem that advocates my living
these hours as the miracle they are—

gems, reminding me to dwell,
as often as I can remember,

in wonder. Right now, that's sharing
the sunset with blackbirds lined up

on the high wire, later in the company
of cooing owls and a full-to-bursting moon.

What Takes Me Back

A sip of cranberry juice
and I remember:

soothing reassurances,
being lifted onto gurneys,
into ambulances,
to and from airports,
the icy rain.

How I had much more
to pray for than my own life.

And after he was taken
to an incubator in the NIC unit,
so small, but strong and healthy,
back in my hospital bed
I couldn't stop asking myself,
did that really just happen?

How one minute you can be
a certain person
and later that same day
someone else entirely.
We had been very fortunate;
that, I understood.

Lights dimmed, the kind nurse
asked if I was thirsty.
All I could think to ask for
was cranberry juice.
Tart and, oh, so cold,
it had never tasted so sweet.

Fortunate

for Allen and Elena

Think about what can happen,
or not, when a woman
makes the naive decision
to become a mother.

Really, it's a leap in the dark
whether a single egg
of the four hundred or so
bestowed in her lifetime

will be in the right place
at the perfect time.
Oh, the euphoria that brings—
the secret knowing

she cradles a new life within.
She walks through her days
appearing to be the same
person, but she's utterly changed,

imagining the budding
heart beginning to beat
in rhythm to hers, praying
that the embryo will grow strong,

and then, not too soon or too late,
make its steady way
down through her portal
into an awaiting world.

Fortunate, to the moon and back—
how I tell my daughter
I love her—that this parade
of miracles happened for me.

Planted

We planted the sycamore tree
twenty-nine years ago,
the boy thirty,
the girl twenty-seven.

Another lifetime, really.
And yet, I can still see the saplings:
thin trunk with shiny leaves,
clinging to the container;
the boy—his mischievous grin,
the way his eyes sparkled
in love with this world;
the girl—a mother before her time,
only wanting to give
and to make sure everyone
was taken care of.

The tree is now fifty feet tall,
covers half the hill.
The man—old soul,
strong of body and mind.
The woman—kind friend,
helping others to find their dreams.

How everything changes,
how everything grows. And still,
the roots of those memories
are woven around and around
my remembering heart.

After All

for my mother

She stands stiffly at the sink,
wispy, grey hair hanging
loose, feet hurting,
washing fruit,
chopping vegetables, intent
on preparing another meal
for us, in this house
whose walls
have been a backdrop
for most of my years,

to our striving,
        our finding.

An unspoken peace
now rests between us.
I want to capture this image,
paste it
into a silver locket
that I can clasp around my neck
when I most long
to remember—
mother and daughter,
laughing in the kitchen.

Out of the Blue

One afternoon, my mother asks if there are
questions I want answers to.

Why, are you planning a long trip?
She hasn't gone away in years.

"Maybe, let's pretend I'll be traveling
for some time." Startled,

but playing along—*do you remember
my huge cardboard box of books, the ones*

*I kept in my attic bedroom in our little house
in the woods?* After a moment of thought,

she responds, "kind of."
Didn't you ever go up there? I tease.

Truthfully, I remember her climbing the stairs
with wet, warm washcloths on mornings

I'd cry out, my eyes stuck shut
from repeated infections.

"Well, I did run up there when our house
caught on fire to rescue the cat

sleeping on your bed!"
I also remember that day and how

I was safely outside behind the water tank
holding my baby brother when she went back

in for the cat and to call the forest rangers.
Now, she wants me to cut her current cat's nails.

Then, we go outside to see how much the avocados
and lemons have grown on her cherished trees.

Returning to the house, I ask, *you're well, right?*
No more symptoms? "I'm fine. Well, mostly I'm okay."

Getting ready to leave, I tell her, *wait to take*
that trip you're going on, please.

She laughs. We hug and wave. My parting words—
I'll think of more questions to ask you.

My Biggest Fan

My mother calls to tell me she likes
the ending to one of my poems.
She does read more of what I write
than anyone else,
but she's not always precisely a fan.

Often, she wants to know what I mean
by my words,
or she wants me to accept
that she sees things differently.
Even so, each time I visit
I see piles of my poems
she has printed to show her friends—
that age-old mother-daughter dilemma.

The poem she is calling about
is more flowery than how
I write now, a cliché
about my life being like a diamond,
multifaceted blessings and all.
But no, she says she doesn't remember
this poem from my book,
the one she persuaded me to publish,
which still lies
on her living room side table.

Rather, she has googled my name
and is shocked by the result.
Regularly she complains
how there is no privacy anymore.
But this time she's not concerned
about the photos of me and my poems

pasted on the internet.
She just wants to affirm
what I wrote is true,
I *have* lived a life of being cherished,
especially cherished, by her.

Our Daughter Asks

What is the secret to staying
married for thirty-four years?
We are tasting wines while
on a FaceTime call
from our table for two
overlooking the Pacific Coast
to her New York City apartment.
I hadn't expected this question,
am taken a little off guard.

I don't want to tell her it was luck.
Or that for some reason the goddesses
of fate looked down upon us in favor—
she who is starting to consider
taking the same leap.
So, I say something more reasonable,
but also true,
like how important it is to communicate
your needs, treat your partner
with kindness and respect.
The answer appeases her.

This morning of our anniversary,
we have driven north up Highway 1
past a herd of elk, past zebras
in the field below the castle
(yes, in California), hiked
to a small waterfall near the point,
stopped at a beach we'd always driven past.

After our picnic, we head south, back
toward home, pass the seaside hotel
where we spent our wedding night.
Do you remember how wasted you were?
This makes us both laugh.
To have drunk that much, either
you were the happiest man in the world,
or you worried you had made
the biggest mistake of your life.
He doesn't respond, just smiles.
It's okay, I know the answer,
have known it all these years.

What Goes Unsaid

As we lie awake talking
late into the night,
what weighs heavy on my chest,
yet I am not able to voice,
is the probability one of us
will someday need to
continue on alone.
Medical history, statistics,
and our ages suggest
it might be me.

It's beyond my imagining.
No more massaging
of sore muscles after a tiring day.
No bodies melding into S curves,
arms and legs intertwined,
like we have slept for decades.
No longer to be held
by the solid trunk of him.

I want to ask how this parting
could even be possible.
And still, I am afraid to speak
those precarious words
into the unspoiled air.

Opened by Loss

"Sometimes breaking brings a gift we didn't know we needed..."
"Anti-lament," Rosemerry Wahtola Trommer

I was forty-nine when my father died.
It was sudden—one afternoon
we were playing cards, laughing and joking.
The next morning, he was gone.
No chance to say goodbye.
Or to tell him he was loved
and a great dad despite struggles
that had torn at the fabric of us.
Trained as a fighter pilot
in the Second World War, I knew
he had been surprised to live into old age.

When I was eight, we planted a grove
of tiny pine saplings together.
I suppose Minnesota was promoting
reforestation that year.
Not long after, we moved cross-country.
More than twenty years later,
when he and I returned to our old home,
we stopped beside the county road
to take a photo of him dwarfed
by those trees morphed into giants.

What I want to say is when a loved one
passes, our appreciation of the life
experiences they endured often soars.
From this humbling loss, I was launched
into being a fuller, more open human.

How Not to Take in Fear

Find a quiet path to walk alone.
See how ocean waves roll
with the pull of a capricious moon,
and the ancient oak holds
ground in a thrashing wind.
Fling praise up to vultures
circling overhead.
Bow like nature to the coin
tosses of circumstance.

Consider a tree for a confidante.
If the journey leads to water,
count on faith to help you
swim safely to the far shore.
Climbing a tall mountain
is a great remedy for fear;
stride upward until you feel
the generosity of Mother Earth.
New muscles will gently evolve,
proving you are stronger than any fear.

A Doorway

Many of us attend to death's distant call
like hearing a train whistle
on the outskirts of town,
unable to picture the pale rider
pulling into the station.

A quick nod of recognition,
then we are distracted
by the panorama whizzing by.

Anticipating loss, I watch a doorway
to death squeak open—
no longer able to disregard
what I previously ignored,
no longer able
to go about my days
as if this existence will never end.

Sleep brings a desired oblivion
where for a few hours I forget
the slow progression of demise.

Mortality now commands my attention.
There is no place to hide,
no other option but to respond
to the persistent knocking,
welcome the guest in.

Dear Friend

for Reverend Robert Lee Norton

You, who were like a father,
a constant factor, mentor and friend,
from adolescence on through motherhood
and middle age, nearly forty years—
how could I conceive of a life
without you here?

As I sit in this medical center today,
waiting for a routine exam,
my thoughts travel to the time
I brought you here.
Whatever it is, you told me,
I am not afraid.

That day, in this same room
when they called your name, I didn't wait.
Instead, I walked downtown
to pass the time.
Was I oblivious? Or just innocent
of time's precious edge?

How I wish I'd stayed and prayed
with all my might.
How I yearn to take the country road
leading to a cup of tea
and the open exchange of a friendship
a long time in the making.

How could I have fathomed then,
that within weeks I would be sitting vigil,
slipping morphine between your lips,
that I would have to let you go?

What it all comes down to in the end

is learning to let go.
Just when you begin
to get comfortable, along comes
another heart-wrenching goodbye.

Being forced to release
my tenuous hold
on one I love and withstand
an uprooting storm
of impending separation,
I find myself trying to fill a hollow
that cannot be satisfied.

Often, even with the heavens
blue to the horizon,
I hear the distant thunderclaps
of squalls to come.

Pushed to delve deeper
into my practice,
into what it means to carry on,
I slowly begin to feel
a little lighter, the band
around my heart a little looser,
my breath a bit easier.

In a way, we are all preparing
to depart,
each of us under the same sky
raining unstoppable change.

To Leave This Plane Gently

As I am being shown how
to leave this plane gently,
there's no need to find a solution
to what isn't meant to be solved.
How useless it is, attempting
to thwart an innate process
wise beyond my understanding,
one that asks only to be honored.

At sunset, a coppery swirl
of brushstrokes, and afterward, the stars
fixing us in a filament of belonging.

Of course, everyone wants a miracle.

What we often get instead is the cosmic
irony of chasing a chimera
that comes in and out of focus—
the divine caprice
of agreeing to exist
at this time and in this space
on our enchanting, perplexing planet.

Tsunamis of unknowing,
portals to possibilities,
and the heavens quivering light.

What I will remember

is how closely death resembled birthing,
and after the last outbreath,
a crow perched in the crown
of the sycamore
proclaimed loudly
letting the kingdom know
one of their own
had fulfilled his sacred mission.
My mother's intuition
made her call at that instant,
she who is likely closer
to the veil and now more easily
senses these mysteries.

For months I prayed
for your passing to be easy
and quick, or if not quick,
at least in your or God's good time.
Only after are we able to see
the gentle way everything fits together,
feel thankful for the precious gift
of a genuine love
and the perfect mentoring
of how to depart from this place.

Time Left to Give

A woman sits at a bonfire
on a quiet beach waiting for me—
she who has made me all that I am.
Maybe I should have given more,
I say to her. *Does the opportunity
continue into the next world?*

She opens her arms, holds me
like her long-lost child.
Taking my hand, she leads me
to the water's edge,
and we swim in sure strokes
to an island not far from shore.

There she tells me I am not yet done;
I will have many more years to give.

Share your whole heart—
with the plants, animals, and people,
no matter what happens.
She urges me to let life sift
gently through my fingers.
To be in love with the world,
and when the time comes, release it.

Once more in my earthly body,
I continue to feel her embrace,
her soft hand, the lulling of waves,
knowing one day I will be her.

wherever we look, the chance for wonder

Abundance

Morning light bathes
my face and filigrees
the edges of leaves like halos.
The soul-stirring cry
of a red-tailed hawk rings
out as she flies searching
across the sky.
If I close my eyes,
I hear a gopher chomping
roots; lizards scurrying
from bush to bush;
a sparrow scratching
the dirt for grubs.
Bees buzz behind my chair
as they dust pollen
from succulent blossoms.
Hummingbirds whiz by
my shoulder at full throttle.
A distant wild turkey
calls forlornly for his mate,
and other bird species
converse in languages
I don't yet comprehend.
Even the far-off hum
of a car down on the road
and faint voices
from the other side of the valley
play across my awareness—
sights and sounds
of a perfectly abundant life.

Ocean Love

Let me not forget to notice
all the seasons of the ocean
with an awe-filled soul—
equally winter's pounding surf
and summer's gentle swells.
Every bay a changing alchemy
of colors—smoke, sapphire,
aqua, slate, and sky.
Let me not forget to search
September's waters
for the curved backs of whales,
their tails breaching toward the sun,
dorsal fins of dolphins undulating
smoothly in and out of waves
just beyond the breaks.
The ocean's briny smell
fills my lungs with longing
for a simpler life.
She urges me to set my cares aside,
float at peace in her salty arms.

Because I brought you here

after "First Fall," Maggie Smith

there is so much I hope
for you to know.
So, I point to things and say—
pay attention to the mist
as it rests on the ocean's surface,
how its radiance transforms
by the second.
Look at that man,
how he gently converses
with the child;
this is true masculinity, a reverence
for innocence and life.
Notice the barn owl visiting
at dusk, who recognizes
that your vocal chords resonate
to the same tones his do.
See the teenager whose ensemble
and hairstyle tell a story
of how she heeds
her own guiding light—
what courage and grace
in today's age of followers.
Greet the jackrabbit
living under the garden cart;
even though she was taught to fear,
see how she perks her ears
toward you in longing
of forgotten oneness.
I so want you to see
the perfectness of how we fit
together—the wonder of this world.
Because I brought you here.

Sacred Hour

Sometimes when I wake
in that sacred hour of deep night,
my life feels perfect—
my longtime love curled around me,
our fingers and feet touching,
the two of us wrapped warmly
in a bedroll of soft sheets.

Through an open window
I hear wind whistling
through the eucalyptus grove.
Then suddenly, a cocoon of silence,
nothing stirring, not even a leaf—
no prancing fawns
eating their way along the berm,
no birds, not even the raucous scrub jay
with her nest of hatchlings
in the ruby-colored bougainvillea.

It's long past the tranquil lullaby
of an owl that perches in the oak
as darkness descends.
Still, the fullness of what is right
is enough for me
to drift back
to the land of dreams.

To See New

Wherever we look,
the chance for wonder.
From my desk, I spy
two white-spotted, spindly-legged
fawns frolicking under the mulberries.
When I speak to them gently,
they rotate already-large radar ears
toward me in curiosity,
then bound off into the oaks
after their mother.
Oh, to live seeing everything
so new, inquisitive
about all earth's inhabitants,
all earth's smells,
imbibing leaf and fruit and petal,
learning what to trust
and what is best to leave be,
to have a free-flowing body
to experiment—
one that prances and sprints
across grassy hillsides
and vaults over fenced orchards,
eyes drinking in the blue, blue sky.

Rain

Miracle of miracles, I wake to rain.
A dousing to quench the smoldering
land and purify the smoky air
after months of fires.
Not just a quick sprinkle,
rather a steady, calming
letting down of clouds.
It seeps into my morning meditation,
and I give extra thanks
for showers of grace.

My body wants to feel sky's caress
on bare skin with little covering—
no underclothes, no jacket, no shoes,
not something the conventional me
would normally do.
I give the eager child permission,
pull on shorts and a top,
leave my hair loose and uncombed,
walk with bare feet onto the grass,
over patches of dirt, now muddy,
and let it all soak in—

the amber leaves
that in my sleep have fallen,
the startled deer,
curious but alert to my passage.
Everything washed clean.
Oh, the glory of being bathed
by a life-force so openhanded as heaven.

Galaxies

In the *Smithsonian*
I read about
a new telescope
that will allow scientists
to virtually explore
twenty billion galaxies.

I picture *Star Trek*
on steroids.

And here
we are yet unable
to figure out intelligently,
heartfully,
how to adequately
take care of our one.

Our Earth

Hardly anyone walks
barefoot anymore.
The crucial connection
has been broken
between the earth and our feet.

In a story, an indigenous woman
tells a fair-skinned child,
take off your shoes; they will make you sick.
He doesn't understand why—
his feet too tender to roam
without sneakers,
his generation oblivious
to nature's healing gifts.

We are electrical beings who need
Mother Nature's energizing charge.

They say if we walk shoeless
on sand, grass, even bare dirt,
our blood flows easier,
our cells swim more freely.
Inflammation is released,
sicknesses cured—
from merely letting the power of the Earth
pulse up through our bodies.

This kinship I have known
for a long, long time.
My soles belong
to the wooded forest,
to the waves, to the powdery shore.

Whatever Name You Give It

after *You Are the Placebo*, Joe Dispenza

Our intelligent universe,
whatever name you give it,
loves us into being,
surrounds us and is within us—
omnipotent, omniscient,
and omnipresent.

Because of it, our hearts beat
a hundred thousand times each day.
Two gallons of blood pump
though our bodies per minute,
traveling a distance of sixty thousand miles
within a twenty-four-hour span.
Seventy trillion cells perform
hundreds of thousands
of essential functions per second.
We mindlessly breathe
two million liters
of oxygen daily, distributed
to each cell in an instant.

This same power that creates
galaxies, and orchestrates the rising
and falling of tides, offers
the miracle of a vessel
that can carry on
for decades,
embracing us wherever it is
on this Earth we stand.

Puttaparthi, India

It's our last morning in the ashram,
home to the late Sai Baba,
renowned guru of mystical healings
and manifestations.

After an Ayurvedic treatment—
herbal medicine patted into
an injured shoulder
alternated with hot oil massage—
I am running late.

Hailing down a rickshaw,
I am delivered to the ashram gates,
walk hurriedly to gather my bag,
past the gilded temple where
we attended *samadhi* and sat in prayer.

Quickly, I run across the street
to eat a potato-filled *marsala dosa*,
drink fresh lime juice, and
order an almond cake to go.

Close by, friends are buying spices and silver.
A moonstone bracelet catches my eye.
Looking nervously at the time,
I pay for it, knowing the bus
is leaving soon for Bangalore.

A man approaches me
as I'm departing from the shop
and declares, *you have a golden aura.*

As you touched each piece
of jewelry, it glowed.

Rushing, but not wanting to be rude,
I bow, mumbling *namaste.*
As I sprint to the bus,
he gently calls out, *it means*
you have a gift for healing.

The First Time I Felt the Energy Flow

Pulsing
sensations
come out of
nowhere, a bubbling
brook from feet to
heart, then
flowing like
rushing
spring water
down arms and
out hands. Impossible-
to-conceive waves
of energy travel
like earthquake
tremors
originating
in some small
southern country,
making their way
through the Earth's
crust to another distant
continent. A seismic
shift so profound,
with aftershocks
lasting for
days. I
sense my life
is about to change,
will never, ever
be the same
again.

Touch

Hands with knotted palms,
where fingers begin to pull
inward like my father's
and my brother's did,
reach out, wishing to ease
my dear friends' pain.

As I dry tears from the weary
faces of my fellow humankind,
I understand dread,
that uninvited guest,
unwashed, dressed in tatty clothing,
knocking on our hidden doors,
pressing to be taken in.

Compassion rouses the pulses
of creation's life-force
to flow from heart
through hands—
my way to love the world.

That Space

Asleep with the senses awake—
that liminal space between
drowsiness and dreams
where the energy takes me
time and again.

Minutes move slowly,
life at a standstill, nowhere
to be, nothing to do, only
inhale and then gently
exhale again.

In a pocket of unknowing
from which creation springs,
I let go
of what I think I know,
unlearning and looking again.

Saying yes to uncertainty,
trusting in the mercy
of a guiding source—
a wink of assurance that
there's time left to get it right.

Full Moon Over Elfin Forest

The opportunity for new insight
can so easily pass us by—
that potential opening to life lost.

With this in mind, I pull on
long johns, then sweatpants,
turtleneck layered with a fuzzy sweater,

knit scarf, puffer jacket,
my daughter's alpaca hat
with braided tassels.

And I make my way to the trees
by the estuary, tiny flashlight in hand,
walk silently over wood planks,

through the forest of miniature oaks,
halting to quiet my thumping heart
when unseen animals scurry in the brush.

Soon, a buttercup moon rises
over a distant hill's rounded breast,
huge and brightly illuminating

the dusky night woods. In that sudden
stillness, only rhythmic sounds
of frogs, some crickets playing

their mating songs, the crashing
of waves on a barely visible shore.

With Venus and Jupiter shining

down on me as well,
I drink dippers of blessings and
give thanks for also being of this world.

Tiny oak

a mere ten inches tall,
I wonder what you are feeling.
Rescued from the shadows,
placed tenderly, tap root intact,

in a new five-gallon home
with the best potting soil
to be found, in a spot
where you will have

afternoon sun,
where you will be seen
and generously tended
with cups of water

when your soil is dry,
until you are old enough
to be planted up on the hill
with the other oaks and pines.

Are you sad to be pulled up
by the shovel's cold steel,
stolen from under
your mother's arms,

where you planned to spend the rest
of your days, little understanding
there was not enough space
or light for you there?

I See You More Clearly Now

One hundred and sixteen souls,
counted with care,
my inspiration
on a quiet afternoon—
to get to know
those who live around me.

Mostly oaks, some spindly
and just beginning,
others like grandfathers
with wide open arms.
A towering pine,
miniature Christmas tree
from twenty-five years ago.
The sycamore planted
before our daughter was born.
An elm that shades
where we sit on the patio.
Mulberries lining the driveway,
their leaves dessert for the deer.
And a small eucalyptus grove,
with trees tall enough for hawks to nest.

To each I say, *I see you.*
I honor your presence
and gritty patience
with battering winds,
sunbaked earth,
birds that squawk and titter
from your branches.
Being the guardians

that you are, I can believe
you love all of this.
Beautiful, sacred trees,
I see you more clearly now.

Plumeria

I have just settled in with a blanket,
cat on my lap,
book in my hand,
when I hear the bells ring.

Four Tibetan brass bells
bought at a yard sale,
etched with intricate designs,
strung on a sturdy green cord,
that I hung on the small plumeria tree
in a pot by my writing room door.

I read somewhere that deer skitter
when they hear wind chimes,
and this was the closest I had.
The tree we have tended from a cutting,
lovingly moving it to larger
and larger containers.
Recently placed in a new planter,
it is being eaten alive.

Already I had given up
the roses in front,
the blue-flowered hedge,
the agaves, whose petals
have mouth-sized bites taken
from their tips.

This time, they've gone too far;
the plumeria was perfect—
dark green leaves,

now a third eaten,
long, thin purple buds
opening into white blossoms
with yellow centers
that perfume our doorway.
Or should I say, used to perfume.

I run to the window to look.
There he stands chomping away
in broad daylight,
no shame at all,
his sweet feast accompanied
by the chiming of bells.

The Spectators

As the sun begins to set,
on the highest tips of leafless twigs
are perched at least fifty blackbirds,
all facing toward the setting sun
and trilling.

Why the sycamore today
and not the almost-as-tall
mulberry trees or oaks?
The best view, perhaps,
or as close to heaven as possible.
At other times, I see their small bodies
strung out side by side
on the telephone wire
in the hastening dusk.

The birds remind me of beach walkers
at this time of day
stopping to face westward.
It's as if watching that sinking globe
is a sacrament not to be missed.

Keeper of the Cave

I didn't take her photo. Or throw a rock
in her direction to scare her
off the path as was suggested.
Though I *did* experience a moment
of fear at such closeness.

Instead, I sent a prayer
for peaceful passage, waited patiently.
As she slithered slowly off the trail,
I admired her splendor—
long, slender, fit, uniquely designed
in camouflage desert colors.
In wonder, I watched as the legendary
rattle slid last into the bush.

I felt the snake had blessed me.
With respect I climbed down
from the rocky ledge,
stepped lightly on the red dirt
where she had been
just seconds before, walked
gratefully back to the trailhead
past juniper trunks
twisted in whirling spirals.

The cave I had visited was her home.
She had allowed me entrance
into this mountain carved by time
as an elder tolerates
the trespasses of a wayward child.

Vultures

Preparing my morning coffee,
out the kitchen window
I see how a needed rain
has bathed our thirsty earth.
Up on the hill, an unexpected sight—
seven carrion-seeking birds
perched in an intimate cluster:
on a roof ridge,
nearby power poles,
tall treetops.
One by one they spread
lofty wings, endeavoring
to dry their appendages
from last night's soaking.
Although at the moment,
there is no sun,
no wind,
no rain,
only a clarion unfolding
to the new day's meager light,
and their trusting it will be enough.

No-see-ums Speak

We rode in on the seaweed
when tsunami waves
covered the sand, made
a home beneath the wet
grains waiting to ambush
you and your friends.
We like sweaty bodies,
warm, dark, snug places—
under waistbands, bra straps,
even the little crevices
of belly buttons
and forbidden bikini lines.

You won't see the results
of our visit until it's too late.
In return for a taste of your blood,
which we need to reproduce,
we offer prolonged discomfort.
Only when hot shower water
hits your body, will you realize
we were there on the beach
you just came from,
secretly invading
while you rested
innocently on your towel.

The Unexpected Guest

On the first day, the lizard greets me
at the front door, but on the wrong side.
After ushering guests in, I return.
By then the lizard is gone.

On the second day, the lizard waits
for me at the bedroom door.
I go to grab the dustpan and broom,
but the lizard has hightailed it out of sight.

I try to enlist my cat
to join the *free the lizard* movement.
He's utterly uninterested in my pet project,
wanting only treats and sleep.

On the third day, the lizard scurries
out of the office closet to say a quick hello.
I catch him with the pan, but he high dives
and dashes behind the filing cabinet.

I wait patiently, speak to him gently
in calming tones. Then success,
one lucky lizard finally repatriated
to his home in the great out-of-doors.

Last day of January

and yet spring is galloping
over the velvet hills,
leaving in her wake
a trail of new neon-green grasses
competing like teenagers
to see who is the tallest stalk.

Water rushes down a narrow ravine
to run into the creek bed.
Pale, pixie-faced calla lilies pretend
not to stare as I walk by.
Five sheep call to me
from up on a knoll.
I stop to chat, appreciate
their fleecy sweaters, practical
in the late afternoon chill.

A young boy peeks out
from behind the fence, curious
why I am conversing
with his sheep.
I enjoy talking to animals,
I tell him. He grins happily,
most likely thinking,
finally, an adult who gets it.

everyday holy

A Poem, A Prayer

"some days
my prayers dress up as poetry
as if they are not the very same thing"
Untitled poem, F. D. Soul

To my ear, every single poem
I write ends up
sounding like a prayer.
Blessing, invocation, expression
of reverence, meditation.
Not so much the petitioning kind.
Rather, prayers of thanksgiving.
Prayers for communion.
Especially prayers for understanding.

Poems help me acknowledge
there's so much I don't know.
How wonderful the idea of Source
as muse, so that sometimes
while writing
a small glimpse is given
of the larger canvas.

Poet—
        devotee of life,
    disciple to the natural world.
Other names for curious,
    for seeker,
        for attempting to make
            the time I have here count.

Praise

Praise sunny summer days—
those fourteen-plus hours
of welcomed light.
Consider me wild about
the ocean, the beach, the waves,
and the games we play,
each of us sparkling
like glitter on water
as we dip and dive for a ball.
Praise to warm sand between toes,
the way my body obediently follows
movements communicated to it.
Because I know life
will not always be like this.
Praise seagulls and pelicans,
the occasional osprey—
birds of my heart.
I raise my arms,
call out to them,
as they glide gracefully overhead.
How lucky I am to live
these pristine moments of joy!
Praise to the omnipotent gods
for bestowing
a life so particularly blessed.

A Practice

She worships   alone   in a wooded
valley   found between
the hard-to-scale   mountains   of loving
what is   and   letting go.

At the edge   of a secluded sea,
in the temple of   soft breathing
and equanimous seeing,
she bows   her head   in wonder.

On the altar   of oneness,   she sacrifices
perceptions of wrong   and right
doing,   lights a candle
for acceptance   that ripples out   to all.

My Power

after "To Change," James Crews

Then came the foggy morning
at summer's sad departing
in what is most likely
the last third of my life
when I understood
that no matter how carefully
I orchestrate my living,
a lot of what happens is not
in my power to control.

What *is* completely
within my power
is to meet each situation
with kindness,
with compassion for others
and of course, for myself,
often the most difficult.

To let it go, as they say, to stop
chewing the cud of wishing
for a different action,
another outcome.

So instead, I look at myself
in the mirror and ask,
did you show the world
you care today; was your heart
an open reservoir of love?

The Mountain

after "god of the green door come," Nan Seymour

Disheartened god of the revolving door,
help me to scale
the mountain of worldly confusion
toward hope.

God of innocent deer watching
from under the orchard trees,
of lizards scurrying nervously
on the garden wall, of owls
hooting out their cautionary tales—
protect us all.

Did we not appreciate enough
our precious incarnation?
Are these omens given
so we can alter the manner
in which we tread
upon our earth?
Signs,
sent for our awakening?

God of the whales,
tails breaching beyond the waves,
and of a crimson sun
landing gently on water,

you loved us into being,
you cried contagion,
you lamented corruption,

and yet, we have been oblivious,
unyielding to your call.

God of the revolving door,
we are stuck running in circles.
Please show us a way out.

See me, hands clasped over heart,
        kneeling on the temple floor,
        praying to you now.

Invitation

Our world right now
is not easy to understand.
A shift is transpiring
whose tremors beg
the human race
to become more aware,
to face personal fears
by taking the next step forward,
to treat each other with compassion,
the way bees gently pass
necessary pollen
from flower to flower
and birds drop seeds
for the birth of trees to come.
To trust in our source,
the way a baby clasps
chubby arms faithfully around
her mother's neck.

Can I accept life as it is
without needing something to change?
An invitation, perhaps,
to be my pilgrim-self.
Risk limping into the temple
offering my garnered flaws,
praising the potential
even while encountering
exile and alienation,
not knowing where
our world is headed, and yet
craving that connection,
hungering to give it my all.

Because

"I saw that worrying had come to nothing and I gave it up.
And took my old body and went out into the morning."
"I Worried," Mary Oliver

Because we love so deeply,
there will never be enough days.
Each morning, help me to accept
the hours before me are a gift,

a blessing of the highest order.
Birds sing open-heartedly
even in a questioning sky,
endless strife that just won't go away.

Our period of great uncertainty—
an invitation, possibly, to choose.
The only sensible plan I can see:
sow love and kindness, instead of fear.

Sow love and kindness, instead of fear,
the only sensible plan I can see,
an invitation, possibly, to choose.
Our period of great uncertainty—

endless strife that just won't go away.
Even in a questioning sky,
birds sing open-heartedly,
a blessing of the highest order.

The hours before me are a gift,
each morning, help me to accept
there will never be enough days,
because we love so deeply.

Riptide

Recall being gripped
by the riptide,
the sudden panic
when it seemed Neptune's net
was mightier
than your mortal self,
the sharp awareness
that measured strokes forward
would get you nowhere.

In another place, in another time,
dragged into a pummeling
with Poseidon,
you rack your mind
for what you've learned
from undertows.
That's right, sometimes
a roundabout slant
is necessary.

Out of the blue,
a will surfaces
to hold fear at bay.
You remember
to draw in
the deepest possible breath
before going under.
Now waves wash over
rather than beat you down.

In the end, primordial powers
of spirit

are summoned,
the ones bequeathed to you
at birth
and honed through time.

Contemplating Faith

after "What's in the Temple," Tom Barrett

We can't talk about faith
and make any sense, and
we can't not talk about faith
and make any sense.
Instead, we talk about the weather,
our families, our health,
but really, we are talking about faith.

When I speak the word *faith*,
eyes glass over.
Maybe we have been frightened
by images of a stern man
holding his scroll of commands.

When I say the word *faith*,
I mean a benevolent force
having your back
and the will for good being powerful.
I'm talking about trusting in it all.

Faith—a temple of protection,
God's good time for everything.
I'm talking about everyday holy
waiting for you
as you open the door.

Late Fall

This morning golden mulberry leaves
drop softly from the trees.
Twenty feet from me two does
calmly eat this favorite breakfast,
lifting leaves gently with their lips
as quickly as they release.
One looks up into the canopy
longingly, hoping for more.
Their orbiting ears tilt toward me
when, through the open kitchen window,
I say hello, coffee cup in hand.
They don't flee, understanding
they are wanted here.

Yesterday, my son held up
one of these leaves,
showed me its scalloped edges,
its perfectly positioned veins.
Later, I saw he had placed it
on my small altar,
in front of the black-and-white photo
of my grandmother and her mother,
to one side of Kuan Yin,
conch shell pressed to her ear,
listening for the answer
to a prayer.

Just for today

remind yourself once more,
but gently now,
that fretting about tomorrow
and reliving yesterday's regrets
will not alter their outcomes.
This habit only snips away
the precious present moment
from before your face,
reduces it to fragments
like confetti never flung
in celebration.

Recall the tiny hummingbird
on a branch
above your head,
how she dipped
and cheeped questing
for your attention.
Remember how that flash
of seldom-seen green
illuminated a beckoning sea
as the sun slipped low
beneath the water.

Just for tonight

I release unruly regrets
from my heart,
untether hurt sentiments,
lay willful worries for a time to rest,
so I may sleep at least a bit
the peaceful slumber of innocents.

Accepting Love *and* Fear

Our emotional lives are tugs-of-war
between love and fear.

We mostly fear what we love
will be taken from us;

for better or worse, this duo
is a married pair.

So, how do I learn to rest
in the cupped, open hand

of one and not resist
the tightly closed fist of the other?

Perhaps fear and love
are but flipsides of our existence.

Hello love, hello fear, help me
consent to the perpetual tumble

of your ebb and flow, follow shards
of broken shells left behind to guide me,

allow for your presence
the way the ocean allows itself

to be pushed by the moon's
elemental pull to the shore.

How to Hold Hope

Hope can be a slippery eel,
barely discernible from a distance
through murky water,
nearly impossible to hang on to.

Floating on the ebb and flow
of currents is conducive to hopefulness,
along with a splash of conviction
that if you remain steadfast,
hope will seek you out.

Hope needs to feel you are one
of its tribe, a kin,
that you have the same stripes
and move in parallel ripples.

Once you have located hope,
grip it loosely.
It may depart but will likely return
because of the home you made for it
in the ocean of your heart.

This Poem

I have lost control of this poem.
The reins have fallen from my hands,
the horse I am riding galloping
toward a steep cliff.

I hang on to his mane,
lean my bobbing head
to his ear, softly whisper,
stay calm, we can do this together.

But the horse has other ideas.
He's spooked, determined
to go his own way, wondering
why I am still on his back.

At the precipice, his temperament
settles, he slows, allows me
to reach down to pick up the reins,
turn him finally toward home.

My Muse

after "The Muse Is a Little Girl," Marjorie Saiser

My muse is an angel,
dispatched here with a telegram,
draped in a flowing gown
sewn of golden threads.
She flies in while I am driving
or when I've just turned off the lights
for the night.
She hovers over my heart,
murmuring softly, reminding me
of the promise I have made.

No, my muse is a master
of black magic.
He looks like the witch doctor
from a tacky black-and-white film,
waking me in the dead of sleep,
taunting there is no way
I will be able to remember
the lines he has stingily
handed over,
word by grudging word.

Remember, he heckles,
you applied for this job.
Do you want it or not?

Words

Words give the tongue wings.
Consider spangled, calabash, chiseled—
their mystical conduits
like puzzle pieces
snapping into place.
Say enigma, Osage, interwoven,
cobalt, Camelot, talisman—
they take you to an imaginative
place far from the small
space you inhabit.
Think nouns—portal,
lullaby, rhapsody, Pismo;
adjectives—secret,
crisp, lucid, speckled;
verbs—preen and praise.
Words can save you;
they are rafts
on a roiling sea.
Putting them together is a marvel.
Taste the word pozole—
how it makes your mouth water,
bursts of tones like shooting stars.

Dreaming in Poems

They say when you start speaking
a foreign language in your dreams
you have reached
a whole new level of fluency,
this the payout for hours
of conjugating verbs—
escribo, escribí, escribiré, escribiría,
thick stacks of index cards
written with new vocabulary—
palabra, verso, poema.

In my dreams, I write poetry with eloquence,
lines that feel precise and whole.
Like in real life, I play
with the words passionately
in search of the best mergings,
attempting to manipulate gears of consonance
and assonance, alliteration and metaphor.

My semi-lucid self urges—
hang on to those verses,
try to remember the sequences.
But in crossing back over the veil,
the slate is wiped clean.
Try as I might to hold on,
words written in ephemeral ink
evaporate upon waking.

this shifting alchemy of existence

A Purpose to All

"There is a season turn, turn, turn
And a time to every purpose under heaven"
"To Everything There is a Season," Peter Seeger

We forget this—
everything that happens
has a purpose.
Even the scarred past
that we pick at in an effort
to obliterate its existence.

We may be criticized
for our fragile choices,
and yet we know on some level
what was necessary
for our evolution.
The luminous stitching
that binds together
calamity and good fortune
to make a much-worn garment,
one that fits us better
than any other
and fulfills our unique destiny.

This too is fullness—
what at first was labeled failure
but with introspection we recognize
served us more than we could
ever have imagined.

Someday

In my daydream wanderings,
sometimes I see into the far away future.
Or possibly not so far away,
we never can know.
Another family lives in our home.
I see children playing in the fields,
climbing trees,
lobbing orchard fruit at one another
like my children did so happily.

An inconvenient necessity,
these years scrolling by—
how everything morphs and changes,
comes to an end. And a new beginning
starts from there.

New hawks will hatch,
fly currents over other heads
as the family gathers, as we do now,
to sit under a canopy of elm.
Perhaps they will appreciate
the hand-painted tiles I chose,
set carefully in the garden wall,
eat the fruit we planted—apricot, plum,
guava, fig, and pear.

There might be arguments,
maybe some cross words, but then
reconciliations under this roof.
I hope the words *I love you*
are spoken often.

I want to be open to saying yes
to that sure thing, that fated
certainty of someday.

I am

not this finite body,
though oftentimes I must
remind myself of that.
I am not the labels
attempting to define me—
daughter, wife, mother,
elder, healer, and the rest.

I have countless questions
no one has the answers to.
I have not found a way
to put an end
to impermanence and change.

There are so many things
I am unsure about,
but what seems totally clear—
I am not done opening
my heart to flower,
not yet finished
with what I came to learn
by means of this unpredictable,
persistent teacher
called life.

Paradox

I am captivated by signs
and weary of constantly
searching for them.
My pockets are plenty full
and empty of the most essential.
Determination and willpower
are my signature dominions
and I want to stop
the world from revolving.
I am exhausted by spouted opinions
and feel the need to share my own.
Give me complete silence
and shower me with the joy
of laughter, the jingle of chimes.
So many last times come too soon
and without change life
would be a lackluster jumble.

The Real Me

I can be a tumbleweed
of melancholy whirling madly
around heart and mind.
I can be inertia
to the hundredth degree,
even with a never-ending list
on my desk ticking for attention.
I can be problematic in a crowd
because at times the truth
as I see it blurts out.
I can be so darn happy on my own.
What I cannot be is perfection,
although I've tried, believe me;
I cannot be someone contrary
to my destiny.
I can be relied on to care,
to help find a solution
when there's a need,
but really, I still have a lot
to figure out
about how to live my own life—
this shifting alchemy of existence,
this paradox of me.

All a woman of a certain age

desires is a full night of sleep,
one the metamorphosis
of her fickle body won't allow.

Maybe instead, she should
give up on the slumber
of innocents, use those hours

when her flock refuses
to be obediently counted,
and memories of floating

in a warm sea no longer
do their sleep-evoking magic,
to have a word with the woman,

or the man, if she sees it that way,
to plead for us malcontents
of the world.

And after whatever compromises
can be made are made,
have a word with the merciful moon.

Spirit

A blustery late afternoon,
both on land and in the tops
of hundred-foot eucalyptus trees
lining the fence—
how do nests stay put
in such wildly swaying branches?

At this height, a hawk
is teaching her fledgling
the art of flying.
The mother hovers steadily
on rushing currents,
the apprentice more daring
in his swoops and ascensions.

When did I begin to lose *my* spirit
of adventure?
The one that steadied me as I dove in
to save drowning swimmers
and encouraged me to fearlessly
explore far-off lands.

Surely, complacency is the most comfortable
choice, but not the way to live
increasingly finite days,
and not what the loved ones
I have lost
would hope from me.

So Many Thoughts

There's something to be said
for the equanimity of youth,
the innocence that keeps them
from thinking too much
about what lies ahead.
Their scrappy resilience to jump back up
after every tumble,
not obsessing over skinned knees—
carefree and on to the next adventure.

These days, I'm an overthinker.
My friend says my mind has more thoughts
than he's ever encountered.
The hyperactivity sometimes weighs me
down, makes me long for
the levity of mindlessness.

Scientists say we have twelve thousand
to sixty thousand thoughts each day.
I must be at the high end.

The inherent promise of a calm mind,
to sit in silent trust on the temple floor—
an invitation to release them all.

Surrender

Will I ever stop expecting
this journey to be a steady row
downstream on sweetly flowing waters?
I should know by now it's a mixed bag.
Wise ones say we seekers
need to surrender—
a manner of living learned with practice.

Like yesterday when I stopped
to watch six wild turkeys
on my usual trek up over the hills.
For months, we had seen a group of seven
roaming in our rural neighborhood.
Now, I counted and recounted,
lamenting the loss of one.
But then the thought—the six
still have each other.
And I tried to take comfort in that
as they clacked along, digging up bugs
hidden under dried leaves.

On my way home, the turkeys
had moved their grazing to the weeds
on the opposite side of the path.
And I sighed with relief to see
once again, there were seven.

Unfixable

This morning, I want to wake
not needing to make
everything okay.
That's me, the ultimate fixer—
forever believing all things
are fixable, and certain
I can find a solution
when no one else can.

I'm beginning to consider
fixing isn't my calling.
As if it were possible to fix it all.
This, I say as I attempt
to crazy glue together
a Mexican planter accidentally
cracked by poking a trowel
through time-worn pottery.

Confident in my abilities,
I don't use gloves.
You can imagine the result.
Now, I'm googling how to get
the darn stuff off my skin.
Olive oil, detergent, warm water,
lemon, fingernail polish remover.
I try them all,
eventually succeed, somewhat.

It's possible I should try to let
unfixable things be.

This doesn't come easy—
it's a mindfulness practice, as tricky
as getting rid of crusted glue
from tender fingertips.

Rebellion of Time

These days I cannot seem to get
a grasp on time.
It's a slippery fish
flipping out of my hands.
It won't be held flat,
like curling edges of photos
left in the sun.

Linear time no longer exists.

It feels like I'm flying high
over sheer cliffs and bottomless canyons
in a three-dimensional nature film.
Precipices come at me from all angles—
front and back,
great heights and plummets,
even bursting forth from inside.

There is no stake to tether time to.

The mythic dragon has slipped
its noose, soars full speed
into the future, caring little
whether or not I hop on.

Loose Ends Undo Me

I want my ducks in a circle,
cellar doors battened down,
unfinished business zipped up,
loose ends tied in a tidy bow.

But life keeps giving me snake dens
full of writhing ends.
Just when one or two are mesmerized
by the charmer,
another three or four go renegade,
refuse to fall under a spell.

I wish for an orderly life,
though sidewinders zigzag
through the grass at my feet.

Tug of War

Lately to my uneasy dismay,
longstanding super-driven me
no longer cares much
about accomplishment
or the weight of things
waiting to get done.

Former good girl doesn't
find this acceptable.
She wants the ultra-achiever
ribbon-winner to return.
She wants the roof re-shingled,
closets cleaned out,
a rich, nurturing stew
simmering on the stove.

New trouble-causer says nope,
to please just let her be.
She takes go-getter gal and sits her
in a corner
to look out the window,
pad and pencil in her lap.

Perhaps what they need
now is to take a stroll
hand in hand beside
persimmon skies, allowing
their metamorphosis
like the changing of tides.

Habit

Recently I've been thinking
about how often I get wedged
inside the wake
of my slow-moving boat,

how many of my days
are maneuvered in much
the same trajectory
as the day before.

A ship that starts to navigate
itself, stuck on auto pilot,
one created from habit
and comfort.

When I consider the times
I've really felt alive,
they were when I sailed
past charted sites,

stepped out on a plank
over a deep abyss, then boldly
plunged into the choppy waters
of the unknown.

What to Remember

What do we want to remember
from this crevice in time?
How division developed
into the norm?
How fear strained to orchestrate
our every action?
The differences that begged
for our allowing?
Or how we began to live
each hour more in appreciation
of the gift,
and this new attentiveness
helped us to shift our inner selves?
What could be more essential
than this?

Progress

I will never understand aggression.
What can possibly be gained
by threatening or harming another
that outweighs the value
of a single life?
It is incomprehensible—
one individual or group wanting
to take from its neighbor.
What emboldens them to believe
they have this right?

Our brains have evolved
at light speed, progressing
technology creating wonders
never imagined in the past.
But, along the way what happened
to the cultivation of our heart space?

On mainstream news, the story
about a Russian soldier—
upon surrendering,
he broke down in tears
when a Ukrainian gave him food
and a phone to call his mother.

What wouldn't we give up
in material advances
to witness more
acts of compassion like this?

Kaleidoscope

As a people, we want this chaotic
time to ease up. So much division
and separation. The life
we have come to expect
quaking under our feet, with
many voicing what we believe
to be absolute truths.

My honest hope—
this stretch of strife
might result in a softer aftermath,
where we live in greater harmony
as tenants of our one world.

Through it all, my heart keens
for peace. And unity.
Integrity, a vital touchstone.
Day by day, I aspire to follow
my own inner whisper
reminding me
no one set of beliefs fits all.

I think about this a lot—
how we are a kaleidoscope
of diverse histories,
races, religions, and identities,
but can we not be tolerant and kind,
remember that which makes us different
is what makes us wholly special?

Scientists say, if you go back far enough,
we derive from the same tribe;
each of us retaining a remnant
of our shared DNA
from some six million years ago.

Clarity

It's a choice,
a declaration to one's self
not to live in fear of _____.
Any dread could be inserted
into that space.
We begin with sensing what is true,
which has its own summoning power.

Like how the deer fixate
on leaves falling
from the tree, looking up expectantly
because they believe
what they want and need
will drop from the sky.

We allow our minds
to be carried away
to a place
where we know not even ourselves.

There are so many ways to die.

Clarity is not a difficult thing.
It's ringing a bell
to call loved ones in
from far working fields.
What if we, instead of terror,
sow the quick sprouting seeds
of compassion
to cleanse
our wounds as they heal?

My Biggest Worry

"The good not done, the love not given, time torn
off unused…"
   "Aubade," Philip Larkin

"My apologies to time for all the world I overlooked
each second."
   "Under One Small Star," Wislawa Szymborska

What do I most fear?
It used to be death,
not because I was afraid of dying,
but when my children were young,
I wanted to be around to show them the world.

Now, I have lived enough to know
with shattering lucidity
things as they are today
will not always be.
This makes me want to soak it all in,
every instant of my precious, precarious life.

I remember. I am present
for a short time.
I forget. I remind myself again.

So, I would say it's a worry
of regretting someday
that I haven't appreciated or noticed enough—
a person, a day, a place,
anything really,
as much as I should or could
at this very moment in time.

The True You

What you will become
I am not yet entirely sure,
but maybe I can lean into
the broken pieces
not yet laid in place
for the mosaic of you.

You have accepted
the sky's invitation,
peeled back the golden seal
of a summons
to show up with all six senses
wide awake, seeking out
the necessary insight
to birth your true self
into being.

I hope you take
nourishment
from the chalice
of clarity,
get as close to trueness
as colored glass gets
to its leaded junctions—
allow that prism of light,
the true you, to shine through.

"The earth, the seas, the light, the day, the skies,
The sun and stars are mine if those I prize."

"The Salutation," Thomas Traherne, 1637–1674

Acknowledgments

As I aspired to write poetry, many special people helped me along the way, and this book is a result of those interactions. When writers began using Zoom regularly in 2020 to offer workshops, I was able to more easily connect with some of the poets I most admire: Rosemerry Wahtola Trommer, James Crews, Danusha Laméris, and Ellen Bass. Thank you for your teachings, support, and mentoring.

A big thank you to Cuesta College and its Emeritus Composing Your Life Story class which I have continued to take every semester for years. In this class, I received my first guidance to write and read my poems, and listening to my classmates' stories never ceases to inspire me. The class facilitator, Sara Roahen, is a gifted writer and teacher, and also the first person to give editing suggestions on this book.

I've learned a lot about revision in two poetry groups—a small central coast poetry group and a Santa Barbara poetry group facilitated by Perie Longo. Perie, I can't look at one of my poems without asking myself, *are there on-ramps or off-ramps?*

I serendipitously found my dear friend Catherine L. Schweig, founder and editor of *Women's Spiritual Poetry: Journey of the Heart*, through poetry. She has become my poetry pen pal and my Reiki sister.

To my long-time friend Lonna Crane, who first offered to let me use her art for the cover of this book and later gifted me with the original painting, I am grateful for our connection and the projects we have undertaken together. Thank you to Alice at Golden Dragonfly for believing this book of poems was a good fit for her press and for working with me to bring it into creation.

To the Arroyo Grande Library, it's like Christmas every time I pick up the books I've ordered. I'm sure I've requested more new poetry books than any other patron through your generous Zip Books program.

I'm extremely fortunate to have a family that supports my love of writing, one of the passions that nourishes my heart. Thank you to my husband, son, daughter, and mother for reading my poems, encouraging me to follow my dreams, and not complaining about the hours I spend writing, revising, and submitting.

My sincere gratitude extends to the editors of the following magazines, journals, and websites in which some of the poems in this collection first appeared. Your support of my work as an emerging writer has meant so much.

Amethyst Review: "Bottom of the Box"

Braided Way Magazine: "Love is an Imperfect Science," "Ordinary Wonders"

Energy Magazine: "Sometimes"

Eunoia Review: "Rain"

Founder's Favourites, Canada: "So Many Thoughts"

Grateful Living: "Ocean Love," "To See New"

Halcyon Days, Canada: "This Poem"

Odyssey Magazine, South Africa: "Because," "Knowing What We Know," "Praise"

One Earth Sangha: What it all comes down to in the end"

Open Door Magazine: "The Spectators"

Pensive—A Global Journal of Spirituality & the Arts: "Accepting Love and Fear"

Quill & Parchment: "Solitaire," "Fortunate"

Rebelle Society: "Habit," "Kaleidoscope," "Our Earth"

Redrosethorns Magazine: "A Purpose to All," "My Resolution"

ROC Metaphysical Magazine: "Clarity," "Time Left to Give," "Touch," "Tug of War," "Whatever Name You Give It"

SLO Review: "Abundance," "Enveloped by the Tides," "Full Moon Over Elfin Forest," "Plumeria," "Vultures"

The Closed Eye Open: "Unfixable"

The Edge Magazine: "Green Flash"

The Mindful Word, Canada: "A Doorway," "Becoming," "Dreaming in Poems," "Enveloped by the Tides," "Humble Praise," "I am," "My Intention," "My Muse," "Paradox," "The Real Me," "To Leave This Plane Gently," "What Goes Unsaid," "What We Want"

Touch Magazine, United Kingdom: "Just for today"

Women's Spiritual Poetry: Journey of the Heart: "A Poem, A Prayer," "How Not to Take in Fear," "How to Be in Love with the World," "Invitation," "My Biggest Worry," "That Space," "The First Time I Felt the Energy Flow," "The Owls' Teaching"

Your Daily Poem: "I See You More Clearly Now, "Galaxies," "Last day of January," "My E-Ticket Life," "No-see-ums Speak," "Tiny oak," "Together in the Evening Light," "Unexpected Guest," "Words"

Anthologies:

The Wonder of Small Things: Poems of Peace & Renewal, compiled by James Crews, "Ocean Love"

Radiating Our Reiki Light, compiled by Rickie Freedman, "Beacon of Peace, Bearer of Light"

www.ingramcontent.com/pod-product-compliance
Lightning Source LLC
Chambersburg PA
CBHW020410150626
46554CB00012B/593